CHRIST'S MIRACLES IN POEMS

Christ's Miracles
in Poems

Ronald E. Hignite

RESOURCE *Publications* · Eugene, Oregon

CHRIST'S MIRACLES IN POEMS

The Scripture quotations contained herein are from the King James Version of the Bible.

Resource Publications
An Imprint of Wipf and Stock Publishers
199 W. 8th Ave., Suite 3
Eugene, OR 97401

www.wipfandstock.com

ISBN 13: 978-1-62564-928-7

Manufactured in the U.S.A.   05/22/2014

Acknowledgment: A special thanks to Diane Eure Hignite for her beautiful painting of Christ.

"The works that I do in my Father's name, they bear witness of me."

JOHN 10:25

Contents

Preface

This book is written about Jesus Christ who has given purpose and a meaning to life for all men. He is the only one who has lived that connects us to our Creator. As it was foretold in the Old Testament, a savior would be forthcoming to the world. Jesus said, "The works that I do in my Father's name, they bear witness of me," and through his miracles he showed others that he was truly the son of God. Without this one life, we virtually have nothing in this world to hold on to regarding the hereafter. He demonstrated in his own death and resurrection that this event is possible for you and me. Who else has lived to give man hope and a promise for tomorrow? There is none of whom I am aware.

In addition to an introductory and a closing poem, there are 36 poems herein that represent 36 different miracle events performed by Christ in the New Testament in the King James Version of the Bible. They are listed as they are found in the New Testament, beginning with the book of Matthew. The scripture under each miracle listed is the beginning location of where the miracle is described. *The Matthew Henry Commentary* and the King James Version of the Bible were used as resources for this work. It is my hope that these poems on Christ's miracles will give others a greater meaning and understanding of his work and deeds, and also be a blessing to their readers.

Foreword

In this book Ronald E. Hignite demonstrates his poetic skills as he describes the miracles of Christ in a clear and meaningful way through poetry and rhyme. The readers will be inspired by the poems in this book and will gain a greater understanding of the divine power of Jesus Christ. These poems represent text found in the New Testament in the King James Version of the Bible. The very presence of Christ is felt in these poems with his words appearing in quotations.

Pastor Gene Williams
Greenville, North Carolina

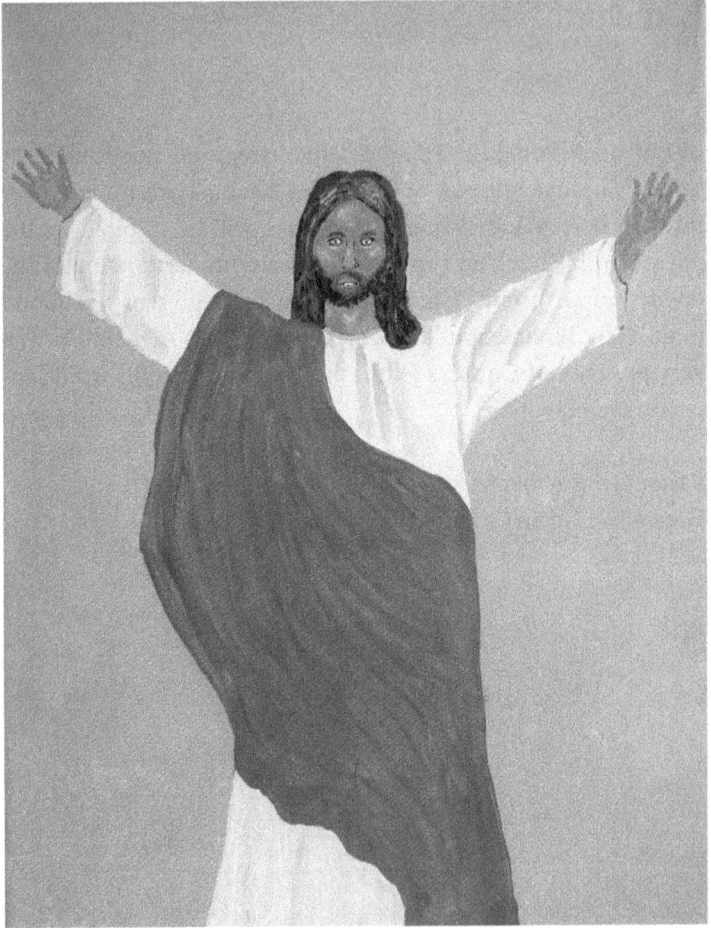

Introduction to

Christ's Miracles in Poems

Christ was born into this life,
And he had a virgin birth.
He was sent here by his Father
To save those lost on earth.

He taught all his disciples
To follow in his way,
And before them performed great miracles
That we now know of today.

Christ came here on a mission,
And through his miracles he would show
That his power was divine,
And from God it could only flow.

...ask him...
...re all things whatsoever
...do to you,
that men should do to you,
...so to them: for this is the
the prophets.
...ye in at the strait gate:
...the gate, and broad is the
...leadeth to destruction, and
...be which go in thereat:
...strait is the gate, and
...the way, which leadeth unto
...few there be that find it.
...ware of false prophets, which
...you in sheep's clothing, but
...they are ravening wolves.
...shall know them by their
...Do men gather grapes of
...or figs of thistles?
...even so every good tree bringeth
...good fruit; but a corrupt tree
...forth evil fruit.
...good tree cannot bring forth
...neither can a corrupt tree
...forth good fruit.
...Every tree that bringeth not
...good fruit is hewn down, and
...into the fire.
...Therefore by their fruits ye shall
...them.
...Not every one that saith unto
...Lord, shall enter into the
...om of heaven; but he that doeth
...will of my Father which is in
...en.
...Many will say to me in that day,
...Lord, have we not prophesied in
...and in thy name have cast
...and in thy name done many
...works?
...then will I profess unto
...never knew you: depart from
...that work iniquity.
...Therefore whosoever heareth
...sayings of mine, and doeth them,
...him unto a wise man, which
...house upon a rock:
...the rain descended, and the
...and the winds blew, and
...that house; and it fell not:
...founded upon a rock.
...every one that heareth these
...mine, and doeth them not,
...likened unto a foolish man,
...his house upon the sand:
...the rain descended, and the

ing authority, and not as the scribes.

CHAPTER 8

WHEN he was come down from the mountain, great multitudes followed him.

2 And, behold, there came a leper and worshipped him, saying, Lord, if thou wilt, thou canst make me clean.

3 And Jesus put forth *his* hand, and touched him, saying, I will; be thou clean. And immediately his leprosy was cleansed.

4 And Jesus saith unto him, See thou tell no man; but go thy way, shew thyself to the priest, and offer the gift that Moses commanded, for a testimony unto them.

5 And when Jesus was entered into Ca-per′-na-um, there came unto him a centurion, beseeching him,

6 And saying, Lord, my servant lieth at home sick of the palsy, grievously tormented.

7 And Jesus saith unto him, I will come and heal him.

8 The centurion answered and said, Lord, I am not worthy that thou shouldest come under my roof: but speak the word only, and my servant shall be healed.

9 For I am a man under authority, having soldiers under me: and I say to this *man*, Go, and he goeth; and to another, Come, and he cometh; and to my servant, Do this, and he doeth *it.*

10 When Jesus heard *it,* he marvelled, and said to them that followed, Verily I say unto you, I have not found so great faith, no, not in Israel.

11 And I say unto you, That many shall come from the east and west, and shall sit down with Abraham, and Isaac, and Jacob, in the kingdom of heaven.

12 But the children of the kingdom shall be cast out into outer darkness: there shall be weeping and gnashing of teeth.

13 And Jesus said unto the centurion, Go thy way; and as thou hast believed, so be it done unto thee. And his servant was healed in the selfsame hour.

Healing a Leper

Matthew 8:1

After teaching his disciples,
Jesus came down the mountainside,
And a great multitude would follow
For with him they wanted to abide.

A leper came upon him
And said, "Lord, if thou wilt, thou canst make me clean."
Jesus touched him and said, "I will,"
As others marveled at what they'd seen.

At once the leper was made clean,
And Christ told him to go his way
To find the priest and testify
He'd follow the commandments every day.

Healing the Servant of a Centurion

Matthew 8:5

Upon his entrance into Capernaum
To Christ a centurion came.
He said his servant lay ill with palsy,
And that his heeling was his aim.

Jesus said, "I will come and heal him,"
And that he would go with him,
But the centurion said he was unworthy
For Christ to come under his roof with them.

He told Jesus just to speak the word,
And his healing would take place.
Jesus marveled at his faith
As he addressed him face to face.

Jesus said because he believed
That it would be done and to go his way,
And the centurion's servant was healed
In the hour of that very day.

Healing the Mother-in-Law of Simon Peter

Matthew 8:14

When Jesus came to Peter's house,
He saw his wife's mother ill.
A fever raged inside her,
And if not altered, it would kill.

Jesus touched her hand,
And the fever went away.
She rose up in front of everyone
And ministered to them that day.

Healing the Sick

Matthew 8:16

As darkness fell in Capernaum,
They came to Christ to see.
They brought to him the sick
And those with demons to be set free.

Jesus healed the sick
And made their bodies right.
He cast the spirits out of those
Who came to him that night.

His actions then fulfilled
What Esaias said so long ago,
"Himself took our infirmities and bear our sicknesses,"
And Christ did this as we now know.

Calming the Sea

Matthew 8:23

As Christ went aboard a ship,
His disciples followed him along.
While they traveled a storm came up,
But Christ who was asleep slept on.

His disciples came to him,
And they woke him so afraid.
Christ said, "Why are ye fearful, O ye of little faith?"
He then arose and calmed the sea coming to their aid.

The men could not but marvel
That the winds and sea obeyed him so.
They asked what manner of man is this
That causes the storms to go.

Healing Two Demon-Possessed Men

Matthew 8:28

When Christ landed in the country of the Gergesenes
With his disciples after the storm,
Two men possessed with devils approached them,
And clearly their anger did form.

They recognized Christ to be holy
As they called him the son of God to his face.
The devils beseeched him that if they be cast
That they be cast to the swine in their place.

Jesus hesitated but little
And said unto them that they go.
As the devils left and entered the swine,
They all perished in the waters below.

Healing a Paralyzed Man

Matthew 9:1

Upon leaving the country of Gergesenes,
Christ traveled back home then by sea.
They brought him a man sick with palsy,
And Christ said, "Thy sins be forgiven thee."

Some thought that Christ was blasphemeth,
And he knew the thoughts in their head.
He told them he said it for a reason,
And then told the man to arise and take up his bed.

Christ told them that he had the power
On earth to forgive all their sin,
And in their hearts they should not feel evil,
But instead be all grateful men.

When the paralyzed man did arise,
The multitude marveled around,
And all of them glorified God
That from this man such power was found.

Raising the Daughter of Jairus from the Dead

Matthew 9:18

While Christ was in Capernaum,
A ruler came to him upset.
He begged Christ to raise up his daughter
Who though dead not leave this life yet.

The ruler asked Christ to come with him
And touch her that his daughter might live.
Christ saw that his faith was so strong
That life to her he would willingly give.

As he entered the ruler's house,
Christ saw the minstrels and did hear their cries.
He went in and took the daughter's hand,
And they all saw his daughter arise.

Healing a Woman with a Blood Disorder

Matthew 9:20

As Jesus walked with his disciples,
A woman came up close to them.
She was suffering from a blood disorder,
And of Christ's garment she touched its hem.

She said within herself
If she could only touch the garment he wore,
That this alone would heal her,
And her disease would be no more.

Jesus turned himself around
And said her faith was indeed the key.
Because of this faith she had showed him,
Her disease would no longer be.

The woman found herself healed
From that same hour on,
And since her faith in Christ was so strong,
The disease that she had now was gone.

Restoring the Sight of Two Blind Men

Matthew 9:27

After healing a ruler's daughter,
Christ departed and went his way.
While he was walking two blind men followed,
And both eagerly had something to say.

They called him the son of David,
And begged he have mercy on them.
Christ said, "Believe ye that I am able to do this?"
They said, "Yea Lord," then unto him.

Christ touched their eyes and he said,
"According to your faith be it unto you,"
And at once their eyes were opened
As Christ then told them what they were to do.

He charged the two men right away
That no man was to know it at all,
But the men instead they would spread it,
And on many ears it would fall.

Healing a Demon-Possessed Nonverbal Man

Matthew 9:32

After Christ had healed two blind men,
He departed with his men,
And as he walked along,
Others approached him once again.

They brought to him a man
Who was both deaf and dumb.
A devil raged inside him,
And that's why to Christ he'd come.

Christ cast out the devil in him
And changed this man that day.
The witnesses had never seen
Such a miracle come their way.

Healing a Man with a Withered Hand

Matthew 12:9

To the synagogue Christ did go
Upon the Sabbath day,
And as he entered in,
One with a withered hand did come his way.

They questioned his healing on the Sabbath,
And if indeed that it was right.
Christ said if he could help someone
That it was lawful in his sight.

"Stretch forth thine hand,"
Christ said straight out to him,
And his withered hand was healed
Right away in front of them.

Healing a Demon-Possessed Blind and Dumb Man

Matthew 12:22

They brought to Christ a man
Whose healing they did seek.
He was possessed with a devil
And could not see nor speak.

From this devil Christ did free him,
And his life would change that day.
To their amazement he would speak,
And his sight was now okay.

"Is not this the son of David?"
The people said who were around,
But still there were those like the Pharisees
Where disbelief in Christ was found.

Healing the Sick and Feeding Five Thousand

Matthew 14:13

As Christ traveled to a desert place,
A great multitude came his way,
And out of his compassion,
He healed the sick that day.

When the evening then had come,
His disciples came to him,
And said the multitude should go now
For there was no food for them.

Jesus said, "They need not depart;
Give ye them to eat,"
But the disciples said they had just five loaves,
And the two fishes was all the meat.

He said to bring them to him
And told the multitude to sit on the grass.
He blessed the five loaves and two fishes
And told his disciples to feed the mass.

Five thousand and more were fed that day
As Christ's disciples carried out his word,
And those around were amazed
Like others when they heard.

Walking on Water

Matthew 14:22

After feeding all the multitude,
Christ remained to send them away.
He told his disciples to go ahead
And take the ship that day.

To the mountain Christ did go
After bidding the mass farewell,
And as he prayed alone,
Darkness upon him fell.

Later Christ appeared to his disciples on the sea,
And when they saw him they had fear.
"Be of good cheer; it is I; be not afraid,"
Christ said for all to hear.

Peter answered back
And asked if he might join him too.
Christ told him to come along
Which Peter then would do.

As Peter walked out to him,
He feared the wind and was afraid,
And as Peter began to sink,
He asked Jesus for his aid.

"O Thou of little faith,
Wherefore didst thou doubt?"
Christ said aloud to him,
And Christ with his hand reached out.

When Christ and Peter came aboard the ship,
The winds did cease for them.
"Of a truth thou art the Son of God,"
They all did say to him.

Healing the Sick in Gennesaret

Matthew 14:34

Christ traveled with his disciples,
And they landed their boat in Gennesaret.
When those around knew Christ was there,
It would not be long before they met.

They brought to him their sick
And those who had disease.
Christ would heal them all
And do so with such ease.

They had such faith in him
If they could just touch his garment's hem,
That Christ possessed the power
To heal each one of them.

Healing a Girl Possessed by a Demon

Matthew 15:21

From the coasts of Sidon and Tyre,
A woman of Canaan came to Christ to see.
She said that her daughter was vexed with a devil,
And said, "O Lord, have mercy on me."

At first Christ said not a word,
But then said as she did weep
That he'd been sent unto the house of Israel
To save all its lost sheep.

Then the woman answered back,
Begging deep from within her soul,
And because of the faith that she showed,
Christ made her daughter whole.

Healing the Afflicted and Feeding Four Thousand

Matthew 15:29

Christ departed from Sidon and Tyre
And came to the Sea of Galilee.
They landed and went up a mountain,
And soon a multitude he would see.

They brought to him the lame and the maimed
Along with the dumb and the blind,
And that day Christ would heal them
Which brought peace once again in their mind.

Christ had compassion for them
To his disciples he did say.
He said, "I will not send them away fasting,
Lest they faint in the way."

His disciples said there was no food
In that wilderness to feed the mass,
But Christ gave thanks for seven loaves and some fishes
And broke them for his disciples to pass.

The disciples fed the multitude
As Christ had told them to do,
And four thousand and more were fed that day
With seven baskets left over too.

Healing a Boy Possessed by a Demon

Matthew 17:14

They brought to Christ a certain man
Who kneeled and asked mercy for his son.
He said his son was a lunatic
And asked that healing for him be done.

The man said he'd been to Christ's disciples,
But they could not cure him,
And Jesus said, "Bring him hither to me,"
Which he did in front of them.

Jesus rebuked the devil,
And from his son it did depart.
The child was cured at that very hour
Because of the faith in his father's heart.

Healing the Blind Men in and near Jericho

Matthew 20:29, Mark 10:46, and Luke 18:35

Upon coming into Jericho,
And as Christ from it did leave,
A multitude of people followed,
Desiring healings to receive.

They saw a blind man as they entered,
And two with one called Bartimaeus as they did depart,
And when they heard it was Jesus,
The blind men cried out from their heart.

Each said, "Jesus, thou son of David,
Have mercy on me."
Others told them to hold their peace,
But they cried out repeatedly.

Jesus said, "What will ye
That I should do unto you?"
The men said they desired their eyes to be opened,
And that's what they begged him to do.

Christ said their faith had made them whole,
And their healings would come to pass.
Immediately the blind men could see,
Amazing all the mass.

Cursing a Fig Tree

Matthew 21:18

As Christ traveled into Bethany,
He saw a fig tree on his way.
He observed it had no fruit
And cursed it on that day.

He said, "Let no fruit grow on thee
Henceforward for ever."
The fig tree quickly withered
And from then on produced fruit never.

When Christ's disciples saw it,
They marveled at what they did see,
And Christ said with strong faith and no doubting
That they could do it like he.

Christ also told them when praying
That what they asked for they could receive,
But for that result to happen
That first they must truly believe.

Healing a Demon-Possessed Man in Capernaum

Mark 1:21

While in the town of Capernaum,
To the synagogue Christ would go.
It was there upon the Sabbath
That his message to all would flow.

Such authority he would show
In his teachings on that day
When suddenly a man cried out,
Asking why he had come their way.

The man was possessed indeed
By an unclean spirit inside,
And Christ knew this evil spirit
With this man could not abide.

Jesus said, "Hold thy peace, and come out of him,"
To the man that to him did shout,
And to the astonishment of everyone
From this man the demon got out.

Loud sounds and shaking came forth
From this man that all could see,
And the miracle that happened
It would pass on to you and me.

Healing a Deaf Man with a Speech Problem

Mark 7:31

While stopping in Decapolis,
They brought Christ a man in need.
The man could neither hear nor speak,
And they desired Christ to perform a special deed.

They wanted Christ to heal him
So he could speak and hear.
Christ spit and touched his tongue,
And took his fingers and put them in his ear.

Looking up to heaven,
Christ said, "Ephphatha" or be opened unto him,
And behold the man could hear and speak
Right away in front of them.

Although he told them to tell no one,
They instead would tell it all,
And word of his great healings spread
As on the ears of many it did fall.

Healing a Blind Man in Bethsaida

Mark 8:22

When Christ came to Bethsaida,
A blind man to him was brought.
They desired Christ to heal his blindness,
And for that reason he was sought.

Christ led the blind man out of town
As he held him by the hand.
He spit on his eyes and touched him
And asked if he could now see upon the land.

The blind man said he saw men like trees
Walking there in front of him.
So Christ touched his eyes again,
And then clearly he saw them.

Catching a Great Multitude of Fish

Luke 5:3

As Christ stood by the lake of Gennesaret,
He saw two ships without men in each.
He boarded a ship that was Simon's
And asked him to go out that he might teach.

After preaching to them his word,
Christ addressed what he thought they sought.
He said to Simon, "Launch out into the deep,
And let down your nets for a draught."

Simon said that they had toiled all night,
And they had to bring their net in,
But he said though they had caught nothing,
At his word he would try it again.

Simon let out his net,
And much to his surprise
A multitude of fish were caught
Right before his very eyes.

James and John, Simon's partners,
They were astonished too.
Jesus said from now on they'd be catchers of men
Which is exactly what they would do.

Raising the Son of a Widow from the Dead

Luke 7:11

Christ came to the city of Nain,
And as he approached its gate he did see,
A dead man being carried
With his mother weeping openly.

For this woman Christ had compassion
Since she was a widow and he her only son.
Christ went and touched the bier,
And those with him stopped when it was done.

Christ said to him, "Young man,
I say unto thee, arise,"
And he who was dead sat up
And began to speak before their very eyes.

Then those around were afraid
When they saw what Christ could do.
They said God Himself had visited,
And rumors spread through the region too.

Healing a Crippled Woman on the Sabbath

Luke 13:11

Christ was teaching in a synagogue,
And it was on the Sabbath day
When a woman who was crippled
Just happened to come his way.

Her body was bowed together,
And she couldn't stand up straight.
When Christ saw her infirmity,
For her healing he did not wait.

He said unto her, "Woman,
Thou art loosed from thine infirmity,"
And when he laid his hands upon her,
She was made straight immediately.

Healing a Man with Dropsy

Luke 14:1

Christ went into a Pharisee's house
Which was on the Sabbath day.
He asked those around who were present
If his healing on the Sabbath was okay.

The lawyers and Pharisees were silent
As Christ's compassion for one did show.
He took a man with dropsy and healed him,
And then he let the man go.

Healing Ten Lepers

Luke 17:12

As Christ traveled to Jerusalem,
He passed through Samaria and Galilee,
And as he entered a certain village,
There were ten lepers whom he did see.

The lepers lifted up their voices
And asked for mercy from him.
Christ said, "Go shew yourselves unto priests,"
And they immediately went forward to them.

It came to pass that they were healed,
But only one of them returned,
And that one fell down before him,
Praising him as we have learned.

Christ said unto the man,
"Arise, go thy way;
Thy faith hath made thee whole,"
And the man was blessed that day.

Restoring a Severed Ear

Luke 22:47

To the Mount of Olives
With his disciples Christ would go,
And there he prayed to his Father
So his feelings his Father would know.

Unto Christ and his disciples,
A multitude of people came along,
And Judas, a disciple,
Drew near to kiss him then move on.

"Judas, betrayest thou the Son of Man
With a kiss?" Christ would say,
And knowing what would follow,
His disciples asked should they smite those in his way.

One of them jumped forward
And reacted out of fear.
He smote the servant of the high priest
And cut off his right ear.

"Suffer ye thus far,"
Jesus quickly said to him,
And then reached out and touched his ear,
Healing him in front of them.

Turning Water into Wine

John 2:1

It was there in Cana of Galilee
That a marriage would come to be,
And Jesus would perform a miracle
That his disciples and others would see.

Jesus was told by his mother
That the wine they had was all gone.
His mother then said to the servants
With Jesus they must follow along.

Jesus would say to the servants
To fill with water the six pots of stone,
And the water would turn into wine
As the water would change in its tone.

Healing an Official's Son

John 4:46

On another trip to Cana,
Christ came from Galilee,
And there was a nobleman
Who came to Christ to see.

He said his son in Capernaum
Currently was so close to death.
He begged Christ please to save him
Before he took his final breath.

Jesus would then say to everyone
That without miracles man won't believe,
And then he said to the nobleman,
"Thy son liveth," and his request he'd receive.

The official then traveled back home,
And his servants he met on the way.
They told him he need not to worry
That his son now was okay.

They said at the seventh hour yesterday
Which was the time with Christ he had been
The fever of his son had left him,
And the official was at peace once again.

Healing a Crippled Man

John 5:1

Jesus went up to Jerusalem
And saw both the crippled and blind.
They had come to the pool of Bethesda
For the healing of their bodies to find.

Many thought the pool was blessed,
And it would remove one's infirmity.
So the sick and ill would journey there
With the hope of becoming disease free.

A certain man was there
Who had been crippled for so long.
Jesus said, "Wilt thou be made whole?",
And the crippled man then did look on.

The crippled man responded to Christ,
And said he had no one to help him.
He said with others entering the pool
That he never could get ahead of them.

"Rise, take up thy bed, and walk,"
Christ said to the man straightaway.
The man rose and carried his bed,
And the man was made whole on that day.

Healing a Man Blind from Birth

John 9:1

As Jesus left the temple,
He saw a man who was blind from birth.
Christ's disciples wanted to know
If he or his parents had been sinners on earth.

Christ said it was not for sin
That this blind man could not see,
And now while Christ could be with them
From his blindness he'd set him free.

Christ spat upon the ground,
And of the spittle he made clay.
He then anointed the blind man's eyes
With the clay he made that day.

"Go wash in the pool of Siloam,"
Christ did say to him.
The blind man went and washed as he said,
And his healing amazed all of them.

Raising Lazarus from the Dead

John 11:1

Now a certain man was sick
Who was someone to Christ so dear.
The man's name was Lazarus,
And his home location was near.

Word had been sent by his sisters
For this man Christ thought so much of,
And he told his disciples
He would go there out of his love.

Upon arriving he'd been four days in the ground,
And his body had been placed in a cave.
Martha met Christ and then Mary,
And he told the sisters to show him his grave.

When Christ saw a stone laid upon it,
He said, "Take ye away the stone,"
And as the stone was taken away,
"Jesus wept," and also did moan.

Jesus lifted up his eyes and said,
"Father, I thank thee that thou hast heard me,"
And he said always he knew He had heard him,
But he said it so others might see.

Then after Christ had thus spoken,
He cried out, "Lazarus come forth," to him,
And Lazarus who was bound hand and foot
Straightaway came forth unto them.

Catching One Hundred Fifty-Three Fish

John 21:4

After Jesus' crucifixion,
He appeared to his disciples again.
This was the third time he did it,
And it was from a ship they were in.

It was on the sea of Tiberias,
And they had caught nothing that night,
But when the morning had come,
On the shore there was Jesus in sight.

Jesus said, "Children have ye any meat?",
And they did answer no.
He said to cast their net to the right of the ship,
And when they did the fish did flow.

When Simon Peter drew in his net,
He had one hundred fifty-three fish.
By following what Christ had directed,
He had given them what they did wish.

Jesus told them to come and to dine,
And no one asked who he might be.
Instead, they enjoyed their time with him
For it was the last of him they'd see.

ind saw Jesus
ot that it was

her, Woman,
whom seekest
him to be the
im, Sir, if thou
, tell me where
I will take him

her, Mary. She
aith unto him,
say, Master.
her, Touch me
ascended to my
y brethren, and
nd unto my Fa-
; and to my God,

e came and told
e had seen the
id spoken these

day at evening,
the week, when
here the disciples
ear of the Jews,
in the midst, and
ce be unto you.
had so said, he
is hands and his
disciples glad,
ord.
s to them again,
my Father hath
I you.
iad said this, he

faithless, but believing.

28 And Thomas answered and said
unto him, My Lord and my God.

29 Jesus saith unto him, Thomas,
because thou hast seen me, thou hast
believed: blessed are they that have
not seen, and yet have believed.

30 And many other signs truly did
Jesus in the presence of his disciples,
which are not written in this book:

31 But these are written, that ye
might believe that Jesus is the Christ,
the Son of God; and that believing ye
might have life through his name.

CHAPTER 21

AFTER these things Jesus shewed
himself again to the disciples at
the sea of Ti-be'-ri-as; and on this wise
shewed he himself.

2 There were together Simon Peter,
and Thomas called Did'-y-mus, and
Nathanael of Cana in Galilee, and the
sons of Zeb'-e-dee, and two other of his
disciples.

3 Simon Peter saith unto them, I go
a fishing. They say unto him, We also
go with thee. They went forth, and entered into a ship immediately: and
that night they caught nothing.

4 But when the morning was now
come, Jesus stood on the shore: but
the disciples knew not that it was
Jesus.

5 Then Jesus saith unto them, Children, have ye any meat? They answered him, No.

Closing to

Christ's Miracles in Poems

Christ came to give man hope
That through him there was a way
To find salvation in this life
That would lead to Heaven one day.

He revealed through his miracles
That his power came straight from above,
And the life he lived here was sinless
Where he showed everyone his love.

As he told all his disciples,
At his death he would arise,
And just as he said to his disciples,
What he said they would all realize.